A Soul's Sacred Odyssey

A Sacred Tale of Tests, Triumphs, and Transcendence

Gargi Aggarwal

Made with ❤ on the BookLeaf Publishing Platform
www.bookleafpub.in
www.bookleafpub.com

Dedication

To Adishakti, the eternal source of creation, destruction,
and transformation—
For whispering your truths into my soul and guiding my
steps through fire and light.

To my *ancestors*, the unseen hands that shaped my
destiny—
For carrying me in your wisdom, for speaking through
my blood, and for reminding me who I am.

May this journey honor your presence, may these words
echo your power.

Preface

There comes a moment in every seeker's life when the silence within can no longer hold the weight of untold stories. This is that moment for me.

For the first time, I am unveiling the journey I have carried within me for lifetimes—one woven with divine encounters, shadows that tested me, and awakenings that reshaped my very being. Every word in this book is a piece of my truth, a revelation of the unseen forces that have shaped me since birth.

I was never meant to walk an ordinary path. From the moment I entered this world, the mystical called to me, marked me, and set me on a pilgrimage of transformation. I have held these experiences in silence, guarded them like sacred fire—until now.

This is not just poetry; this is a testament. To the divine that whispered, to the ancestors that guided, and to the soul that remembered.

If you have ever felt the presence of something greater, if you have ever questioned the limits of this reality, if you have ever longed to understand the depths of your own soul—then welcome.

You were meant to find this.

— Gargi

Acknowledgements

No journey is ever walked alone.

To **Adishakti**, my eternal guide—every word in this book
is a reflection of You.
To my **ancestors**, who have walked beside me, unseen
yet ever present.
To my **parents**, who unknowingly nurtured a seeker's
path.
To **myself**—for embracing the fire, for remembering, for
finally speaking my truth.
And to **you**, the one meant to find these words—may
they awaken something long forgotten.

— **Gargi**

1. Born of the Divine

Before I was breath, I was a prayer,
A whisper woven in sacred air.
My mother called on gods unknown,
Each vow a seed in my soul was sown.
At six months, the heavens spoke,
A voice that through the silence broke.
"A soul of light is on her way, Keep your vows—let none
betray."

But fate is cruel to those born bright,
It tests their fire, dims their light.
My mother burned in fever's hold,
While doctors turned their hearts to cold.

Yet through the dark, a voice remained,
A guide unseen, by love sustained.
"Fear not, this birth is blessed and true,
She'll wear a mark—a sign for you."

And when the hands of man withdrew,
The heavens did what heavens do.
No struggle, no cry, no force, no strife,
I slipped into this world—into life.

A birthmark kissed my waiting skin,
A prophecy sealed deep within.
The voice was gone, it spoke no more,
Its final task forever sworn.

A child of light, yet bound by time,
Born with a fate both fierce and divine.

2. Veiled by Fate

I came to this world in a silken glow,
Fair as the moon, with a tongue like a flame.
A mark of the heavens, a story untold,
A child of the Goddess, unshaken, untamed.

"Kaali, Durga" my father would say,
Smiling as if he already knew.
A spirit of fire, both wild and free,
Woven from dusk and morning dew.

The first Navratri, the drums beat loud,
My parents bowed in prayer so proud.
But in the next room, wonder grew—
Dark streaks on hands they never knew.

Ash and kohl traced my face so small,
As if the Goddess had touched them all.
A silent sign, a knowing deep,
A power within me, yet asleep.

And as I grew, my heart would race,
When Navratri's light would fill the space.
On the first dawn, with a heart so free,
I danced in the veils draped on me.

My father would place a new one with care,
And I'd twirl in the old, lost in prayer.
Wrapped in colors, wrapped in grace,
A child of devotion, lost in Her embrace.

Then came the voice, unshaped yet clear,
Guiding their hands in worship sincere.
"Offer this, light the flame,
Sing Her name, embrace Her frame."

But fate is careful with gifts so rare,
To see too soon is too much to bear.
A seer spoke with wisdom untamed,
"Let her sight sleep, or sorrow remains."

And so, they veiled what burned so bright,
Silenced the whispers of second sight.
Yet time will turn, the wheel will spin,
And all once lost shall rise again.

3. Silent Scars

I was sent away, too young to know,
That sorrow moves in quiet waves.
Grief stood heavy on the ground below,
While I was placed where silence stays.

The walls were high, the doors were closed,
Yet shadows crept where light should be.
A child alone, a world exposed,
To things the eyes should never see.

The wind would whisper through the cracks,
With echoes only I could hear.
A nameless storm, a haunting past,
A weight too deep, a shape unclear.

And though I spoke, though words were formed,
They faded soft, dissolved in air.
A voice too small against the storm,
A question left, an answer spared.

Then years would pass, but touch would burn,
Like unseen embers on my skin.
Love would reach, and I would turn,
Still trapped in places I had been.

Yet even now, through veiled despair,
I feel a fire that won't erase.
For though the night was never fair,
It could not steal my light's embrace.

4. When Krishna Called My Name

As a child, I wasn't just me—
I was Krishna, wild and free.
Wrapped in silk, with anklets bright,
Standing tall in temple light.

For seven days, the air would hum,
As sacred verses filled my home.
And every dawn at the stroke of four,
He'd wake me up—playful, sure.

Krishna stood there, teasing me,
With that naughty, knowing glee.
I'd rub my eyes, beg for rest,
But He would never let me rest.

At night, the anklets softly rang,
Echoing where no one sang.
I'd glance at Him, my stubborn friend,
If He ignored me, I'd pretend—

To fight, to scold, to turn away,
But His idol's smile would shift and stay.
From soft to bright, from sad to wide,
A silent laugh, a friend, a guide.

Then darkness came, it pulled me in,
A voice too sweet, a well-planned sin.
One snip—my hair, the strands fell loose,
And every year, I paid my dues.

May and June became a curse,
With fevers, chills, and something worse.
My body weak, my summers lost,
A price I never knew the cost.

But then he came, her fiercest foe,
With fire-lit eyes that burned below.
A chant, a flame, a final fight,
And shadows fled into the night.

Since then, no sickness came my way,
No weight of fear, no debts to pay.
Krishna smiled, as if to say,
"I never left, I always stay."

5. Whispers of Shiva

The temple stood in moon's embrace,
newly born, a sacred space.
Mahashivratri, night so bright,
held me close in dawn's first light.

A vow I made, my first, my own,
to fast for Him, to stand alone.
Yet hunger's tremor broke my will,
a child's body, fragile, still.

Through temple doors, I stepped outside,
where rain and silence would collide.
Streetlights cast their golden hue,
and then I saw—Oh, could it be true?

A shadow tall, with matted hair,
trident sharp and cobra's stare.
No thief, no man, but time stood still,
Shiva had answered, by His will.

I stepped ahead, He stepped behind,
a dance between the soul and time.
One more step—and He was gone,
like mist dissolving in the dawn.

Since that night, the skies obey,
they weep with me, they dance and play.
A whispered wish, a silent plea,
and rain would fall to set me free.

I laughed, I cried before His eyes,
He was my truth, no need for lies.
The only one who understood,
who held me close when no one could.

I called Him Deva—don't know why,
it just felt right, like earth and sky.
And every time I spoke His name,
the winds would shift, the heavens came.

For every hunger, pain, or call,
He answered, watching over all.
And in the rain, I always knew,
Shiva stood beside me too!

6. A Vow to the Eternal

I read of you, my heart swayed deep,
Not as a child, but a soul in need.
Not just the flute, nor playful glance,
But a love that called beyond mere chance.

With trembling hands, I held you close,
Lit a flame, the fire rose.
Seven circles, steps divine,
A vow was made—you became mine.

A childish act, I once believed,
Yet time stood still, the vow stayed sealed.
O Krishna, my love, my call, my plea,
Come to me in form I see.

In dreams, you wed me long before,
Unveiling truth my soul once wore.
Radha's grace, her whispered boon,
A love untouched by time or moon.

No stars align, no fate allows,
For none can claim what's yours, I vow.
A hundred tried, yet none could stay,
For only you shall walk my way.

Even a seer, with sight so keen,
Saw trials where my path had been.
She spoke of storms, of roads unfree,
Yet offered a remedy—meant to be.

"Before you wed, first wed Him true,
Let Krishna claim what belongs to you.
Then no force shall break the thread,
That binds your fate where love is bred."

So, I pray—not for miracles untold,
Not for gods to break the mold.
But for Him, in flesh and breath,
To find me here, before my death.

A love so real, so destined to be,
O Krishna, won't you walk to me?

7. A Love That Wasn't Meant to Be

I was a girl of fifteen years,
Untouched by love, yet drowned in prayers.
And when I saw him, time stood still,
A fleeting glance, a fated thrill.

His voice, his smile—a sacred sign,
Was this my Krishna, my divine?
For three short days, my heart would race,
And in his eyes, I found my place.

But I was young, a child to him,
While I spent years lost within—
Fourteen years of whispered dreams,
Loving him in silent themes.

Then fate returned, the pages turned,
And this time, it was he who yearned.
Yet love was shy, it played its game,
And neither spoke, and none remained.

On and off, for years it spun,
A love that was, yet never won.
For he was torn, yet held me tight,
A shadow clinging to the light.

But Krishna's love is fierce and true,
Not tangled in a world askew.
So when I saw the truth so bare,
That love must breathe, not trap in snare,
I broke the chains, I walked away,
Fourteen years dissolved that day.

For what is real, will always stay,
And what is false shall fade away.

8. Awakening of the Mystic Within

I once walked the road they paved,
The safe, the known, the well-behaved.
Numbers and theories filled my days,
But my heart begged for different ways.

Science was chosen, but not by me,
A world of rules where I couldn't be free.
I buried my dreams beneath the weight,
Of expectations, duty, and fate.

I was a topper, bright and bold,
Yet my soul whispered, this feels cold.
I followed the herd, did as they said,
Yet felt like a bird with wings of lead.

College came, I tried again,
But formulas turned to silent pain.
I knew this wasn't where I belonged,
But breaking free—was that so wrong?

Then one day, like fate's own play,
A woman came, and changed my way.
She spoke of healing, hands of light,
Of energy flowing, pure and bright.

I never planned, I never sought,
Yet Reiki found me, as if I was taught.
No books, no time, no trial, no test,
Yet my hands knew—they did the rest.

It felt like home, like something lost,
Had found me back, no fear, no cost.
Eight months passed, and then once more,
The universe knocked upon my door.

A deck of cards, a whisper deep,
A sight unseen, a truth to keep.
A page was made, a game, a whim,
But destiny had other plans within.

A spark turned flame, a flame to fire,
Each step I took, I climbed up higher.
From healer's touch to tarot's call,
I found my truth—I found it all.

I left behind the scripted ways,

To walk the path that chose my days.
No longer lost, no longer blind,
I stepped into the fate designed.

9. Spells, Shadows, and the Rise of a Healer

I walked the path of men and gold,
Chasing dreams that stories told.
But fate had carved a deeper trail,
A whisper soft, a siren's wail.

The night they spoke of my birth so rare,
A fire awoke, a silent stare.
A hunger grew, a need unknown,
To touch the power I was shown.

So I sat, I breathed, I closed my eyes,
Called the force that stirs the skies.
But the stars fell dark, the air grew cold,
And shadows wrapped their silent hold.

A voice that echoed, a sight so grim,
My body ached from deep within.
The world turned dim, one ear went blind,
A force too wild, too unconfined.

I ran, I stopped, I let it sleep,
But fate had promises to keep.
Seven days, the sacred flame,
And once again, it called my name.

The serpent woke, it coiled, it rose,
Through every nerve, it fiercely flowed.
For once I breathed, for once I knew,
But after seven, darkness grew.

A pain so deep, no healer found,
A weight that kept me to the ground.
They searched, they guessed, they shook their heads,
"How does she walk when life has fled?"

Then fire spoke, a candle bright,
A whisper danced within the night.
A spell was cast, the flame burned high,
And with the dawn, the pain passed by.

The wounds were gone, the chains unmade,
A gift was born, the past repaid.
I once had sought, I once had run,
But now I know—I am the One.

10. The Hidden Scrolls of My Soul

Curious whispers called my name,
A hidden path, a flickering flame.
The Akashic doors stood tall and wide,
A past-life reader as my guide.

I learned the art, I traced the scrolls,
Through time's great weave, through ancient folds.
Yet on one night, in silent breath,
The veil dissolved—no space, no death.

I closed my eyes, was pulled within,
Beyond the flesh, beyond the skin.
Through lifetimes lost, through echoes old,
The past unraveled, truth untold.

I soared beyond the worlds of men,
Through shifting time, beyond the when.
A place so pure, untouched by dust,
Where silence hummed in sacred trust.

And there they stood—Shiva, bright,
Parvati, fierce, in golden light.
Their gaze, a storm, both wild and kind,
Unraveled threads of fate entwined.

"You are ours," they softly spoke,
A fire in me, at once, awoke.
Not by birth, but by a test,
Sent to learn, to earn, to best.

To walk the path, to forge the might,
Not gifted grace, but earned in light.
And Krishna—why my heart still yearned,
A love from lifetimes once unturned.

I fell to knees, my heart aghast,
How could I be what they had cast?
Flawed and lost, a soul untrue,
Yet proof arose in skies so blue.

Through whispered dreams, through signs so bold,
They called me back to truths untold.
Three long years, their love remained,
Until I knew—I had been claimed.

11. The Sleepless Curse

The night was young, my heart was light,
A day of joy, a world so bright.
I held my phone, my gift, my prize,
Not knowing soon, I'd beg the skies.

I laid to rest with dreams so sweet,
Yet darkness coiled beneath my feet.
A sudden gasp, no breath to take,
My lungs betrayed, my soul would shake.

One minute passed, then breath returned,
But deep inside, a fire burned.
I told my mom, then brushed it by,
But fate had plans—I knew not why.

The next night came, all seemed alright,
I laughed and lived without a fright.
But as I lay, my world turned black,
A panic struck, no turning back.

I ran, I wept, I fought for air,
Yet nothing eased the deep despair.
For thirty minutes, time stood still,
No force nor prayer could break its will.

Each night became a silent fight,
A war between myself and night.
Sleep was lost, a distant dream,
I stayed awake, afraid to scream.

The sun would rise, and I would fade,
A creature in the light afraid.
The whispers came, the shadows grew,
The things unseen, I somehow knew.

A curse, a spell, a twisted fate,
A force unseen stood at my gate.
Yet even as the dark would call,
I swore that I would never fall.

12. The Frost That Burned My Chains

The nights grew long, the air grew thin,
A war within I couldn't win.
Spells were cast, the shadows near,
Each breath I took was laced with fear.

The air at home felt cold, unkind,
Like whispers clawing at my mind.
A house once warm, now held my dread,
With sleepless nights and silent dread.

Yet fate had placed within my hands,
A chance to break these iron bands.
A trip arose—a fleeting chance,
To break the curse, to change the dance.

The mountains called, their voices bright,
Where stars would guard my soul at night.
I left behind my mother's hands,
To stand alone on foreign lands.

With trembling breath and weary eyes,
I feared the dark, I feared goodbyes.
But when I slept beneath the sky,
The fear dissolved, the ghosts ran dry.

I laid my head, the silence sweet,
No phantom breath, no restless feet.
For seven nights, I slept so sound,
As if the stars had sung me down.

But fate would laugh, as fate does best,
For peace was brief, a fleeting guest.
I stepped back home—my heart turned tight,
The ghosts returned that very night.

Yet now I knew, beyond those walls,
A world awaited, free of thralls.
And so I roamed where mountains rose,
Through icy peaks and frozen snows.

At fifteen thousand feet I stood,
In biting winds, in frozen wood.
My heart once weak, now burned so bold,
A fire forged from frost and cold.

And though the nights still fought me back,

Though shadows crept and skies turned black,
I knew at last—I wasn't weak,
For I had climbed the mountain's peak.

13. A Wish, A Curse, A Never-Ending Fight

Each year, a wish upon the flame,
Yet every birthday felt the same.
A fleeting joy, a moment bright,
Then swallowed whole by endless night.

One year, my breath was torn away,
Gasping, pleading, forced to stay.
The next, a terror in my chest,
Sleep became a distant guest.

Another year, my body broke,
Jaundice wrapped me in its cloak.
No feast, no cake, just bitter days,
Each birthday cursed in unseen ways.

I ran to mountains, far and wide,
Hoping peace would stem the tide.
The snow, the air, it healed me then,
Yet home returned me to the end.

Books spoke of power in the mind,
Of quantum shifts, of paths aligned.
I leapt through realms, I changed my fate,
Yet the darkness never did abate.

A scent too sharp, a perfume's trace,
Would set my heart in frantic race.
Walls held smells I couldn't bear,
They choked me, gripped me, stole my air.

I ran outside in midnight's chill,
Escaping scents that made me ill.
My brother drove, the air felt light,
Yet dread returned with every night.

The walls still whispered, the air still clawed,
The unseen chains still kept me awed.
I fought, I rose, I burned, I bled,
Yet fate still spun its tangled thread.

Each victory, a fleeting spark,
Yet shadows lurked beneath the arc.
I learned to stand, but never free,
The war still raged inside of me.

14. The Night the Goddess Came for Me

Through sleepless haze, my faith was worn,
Between the prayers and nights forlorn.
Yet in those Navratris, I took a dive,
Into scriptures where Devi thrived.

I read her words, her stories old,
Yet something stirred—something untold.
Visions flickered, a voice so near,
A presence rising, soft yet clear.

At first, I thought, "Is this my mind?"
A trick of longing, cruel and blind.
Yet night by night, she called my name,
Till dream and waking felt the same.

And then it happened—clear as day,
Not in thought, nor mind's array.
Golden light filled up my space,
A glow so fierce, yet full of grace.

I gasped, I wept, I knew her gaze,
As time stood still in holy blaze.
My mother woke and saw me there,
Bathed in light, in something rare.

The moment she stirred, the glow withdrew,
But something changed—I finally knew.
She wasn't just a whispered plea,
That was the night the Goddess came for me.

No longer lost, no more astray,
She held my hand and led the way.
And in my darkest, deepest woe,
Her arms would wrap, and I would know—

That though the world may turn its face,
Though nights may steal my soft embrace,
I am not alone, I never was,
For she still walks the path I cross.

So when I break, when shadows creep,
When silence drowns the will to weep,
She whispers soft, "Child, don't you see?
You were never lost—you are a part of me."

15. The Awakening of the Enchantress

The night still whispered, cold and long,
Yet something shifted, something strong.
The Goddess came, and paths unfurled,
A guiding light within my world.

A teacher came, his voice so wise,
He saw the fire in my eyes.
Through healing arts and sacred ways,
He led me through the darkest maze.

The sleepless curse still held me tight,
Yet now I walked with inner sight.
Once or twice a week, I'd rest,
A fleeting gift, but still, a test.

My soul ignited, power grew,
Kundalini rose in golden hues.
Visions deep and dreams untamed,
The stars above had called my name.

With gifts in hand, I crossed the seas,
A life once chained, now running free.
Yet fate had twists, and storms still came,
Anxiety now burned by day.

But knowledge whispered, secrets old,
I traced the dark, I broke its hold.
No more fear, no whispered dread,
I stood where even phantoms fled.

A girl once frozen, scared to breathe,
Now stood where ghosts would dare not creep.
No chant, no spell, no shadow's plea,
Could shake the force alive in me.

So send the dark, let demons rise,
Let curses fall from jealous eyes.
For now I stand, unbound, untamed,
Protector crowned, my soul reclaimed.

16. Haunted, Hunted, But Never Defeated

The night was still, the air so cold,
A story untold, a fate controlled.
I laid in peace, or so it seemed,
Till shadows stirred inside my dream.

A force unseen, yet strong and tight,
Pulled my soul into the night.
My body froze, my breath grew thin,
A war began beneath my skin.

I leapt, I ran, my feet like lead,
A ghost of me, half lost, half dead.
I stomped the ground, I gasped for breath,
Dancing on the edge of death.

The silence whispered, dark and deep,
"End it now—eternal sleep."
A blade so close, so sharp, so near,
But through the dark, I felt her here.

A voice divine, so soft yet strong,
Sang through my bones, "You must hold on."
The knife fell down, my tears ran wild,
The goddess wept, I was her child.

My brother woke, my mother cried,
He held my hand, we stepped outside.
Beneath the stars, I let it pour,
The pain, the fear, I screamed no more.

To Krishna's feet, I laid my grief,
"End this now, or grant relief."
He heard, he saw, but tested still,
A spirit came with vengeful will.

Three nights awake, no rest, no peace,
No prayer could make the torment cease.
My father watched, his heart in pain,
And then the gods unlocked my chain.

Within two days, a home was found,
A sacred space, pure, safe, profound.
The past behind, I walked ahead,
A life reborn, though fears weren't dead.

The house stood bright, the walls so wide,

The light of Devi by my side.
I never looked back, I never turned,
For in that fire, a soul was burned.

And in its place, a warrior rose,
The night I lived, the path I chose.

17. The Rise After Ruin

One sleepless night, by fate's demand,
My fingers traced through time's cold hand.
A photo glowed—a past so bright,
A girl who knew no endless night.

Her eyes held dreams, so soft, so wide,
Before the storm, before the tide.
I touched her face through glass so thin,
And felt the war she'd soon begin.

I wept for her, for all she lost,
For every scar, for every cost.
For sleepless nights, for battles fought,
For wars with demons never sought.

But as my tears began to dry,
A voice within me dared to cry—
"Don't mourn the girl who walked in light,
For she became the storm at night."

The pain, the dark, the endless fight,
Had carved my soul in sacred might.
The hands that once knew trembling fears,
Now held the weight of warrior years.

But envy lurked with poisoned hands,
Not spirits now, but human plans.
The smiles that hid their sharpened knives,
The whispers clothed in friendly lies.

I felt their gaze, so cold, so tight,
Their jealousy—a venomous bite.
The world I trusted turned to sand,
So I withdrew, unchained their hands.

I closed the door, I shut the sound,
Let silence be my sacred ground.
A month alone, with breath so deep,
I met the self I swore to keep.

Through every wound, through every scar,
I found the truth of who we are—
Not shattered glass, not broken things,
But fire-born, with rising wings.

And when I rose, the earth stood still,
My heart a blade, my soul—a will.

No chains could hold, no curse could be,
For I had learned—I was set free.

18. The Trials of a Chosen Soul

I rose from the depths, a warrior reborn,
With Devi's fire in my eyes, wisdom sharp as a thorn.
Navratri arrived, and the heavens did part,
She spoke through my lips, She burned through my
heart.

The teacher invoked Her, a touch so divine,
My soul held Her presence, Her power was mine.
No longer just labor, no business in sight,
Each healing, each whisper—a dance with the Light.

Yet the nights stood stubborn, refusing to mend,
Not fear, not panic—just a cycle to bend.
A body once shattered, still bearing the trace,
Of years in the darkness, of time's cruel embrace.

But Devi had more, a lesson unspoken,
A trust to be tested, a faith to be woken.
All that I built, all riches hard-earned,

Scattered like ash, as fortune had turned.

Coins disappeared, like whispers in air,
Lent to the past, spent without care.
Five years of striving, now dust on my hand,
A fate I resisted, yet couldn't withstand.

And just as I grieved what slipped from my sight,
A childhood longing awakened that night.
A dream of the heavens, of magic untold,
To chase the green fire in a land bitter cold.

But Russia stood distant, the world's farthest end,
No money, no passage, no way to pretend.
And how would my father, so rooted, so wise,
Let me chase northern lights through the foreign skies?

Yet Devi was watching, Her game yet to play,
For loss is but shadows that birth a new way.
Would I surrender, or would I despair?
Would I trust in Her path, or collapse in the snare?

For the night was still young, and the story not done,
The Goddess had plans, and the Light had begun.

19. Universe Painted My Heart in Aurora Green

One night, in silence deep and wide,
Devi and Shiva sat by my side.
They asked, What is it that your heart desires?
I whispered, To dance beneath celestial fires.

Not just a dream, not just a sight,
But a promise to heal beneath emerald light.
For years of wounds, for echoes past,
To honor the child who wished to last.

But fate was cruel, my pockets bare,
The road was blocked, the path unclear.
Yet every night, in vision bright,
I stood beneath the swirling light.

Then Devi spoke—her voice a tide,
"You will go, I stand beside."
I gasped in awe, my heart in flight,
For she had never failed her light.

Then came a friend, a soul so rare,
Who lifted my dream with love and care.
"Take your time, return it slow,"
She said, as fate began to flow.

With strands of fire, my hair turned red,
Like rising from the ashes, no longer dead.
A woman reborn, fierce and free,
Stepped into the snow, where I was meant to be.

First night passed—the sky was still,
No cosmic dance, no divine thrill.
Yet faith held strong, I knew her ways,
She wouldn't bring me here in vain.

Then, unplanned, when all seemed done,
The heavens cracked—the dance begun.
Green flames swayed, the sky caught fire,
Shiva and Shakti, in love's attire.

My breath was stolen, my body froze,
A surge of something my soul once chose.
Tears spilled forth—not from pain, not from fight,
But from the touch of heaven's light.

My inner child, small and frail,

Reached for the sky, let out a wail.
She wept, she laughed, she danced in snow,
For all she lost, for all she'd known.

And I, the woman, scarred yet strong,
Held her hand, we sang along.
No more broken, no more torn,
Under the aurora, we were reborn.

I left that land, yet not the same,
No longer trapped in fear or shame.
The girl who once only dreamed in the dark,
Now walks in light, with fire in her heart.

20. A Soul's Sacred Odyssey

The new year dawned, and sleep returned,
A fragile gift, a lesson learned.
Yet soon, the silence slipped away,
Nights stretched long into endless days.

Fifty, sixty hours awake,
No dreams to chase, no rest to take.
But fear no longer ruled my mind,
For strength in solitude I'd find.

Then Devi smiled and sent her grace,
A guardian strong, with boundless faith.
Hanuman's name became my guide,
Through every prayer, he stood beside.

For twenty-one nights, his fire burned,
And in its glow, my soul returned.
Fear dissolved, and in its space,
Came bliss, devotion, and divine embrace.

But Devi loves to test my trust,
To forge my faith, to strengthen must.
And so, from shadows, whispers came,
A voice that questioned all I'd gained.

"Is this real, or just belief?"
"Are you lost in self-deceit?"
Her words cut deep, they made me shake,
And doubt within began to wake.

I trembled, wondered—was this all true?
Or was I speaking to myself anew?
But then I stood before her light,
And whispered, bold, with burning might—

"Even if this is madness wild,"
"Then let me be your lunatic child."
"For if my delusion leads to Thee,"
"Then let the world name insanity."

She laughed, she danced, her bells did chime,
"You've passed, my child, now claim what's mine."
And in that glow, a path unfurled,
A guiding force within this world.

A Guru's voice, a whispered call,
A bridge to Her, beyond the wall.

With every step, through sacred flame,
He leads me deeper in Her name.

Yet this is not where the tale will cease,
For grace unfolds in endless peace.
The journey hums, the fire burns free,
This is just A Soul's Sacred Odyssey.

21. New Poem

www.ingramcontent.com/pod-product-compliance
Lightning Source LLC
Chambersburg PA
CBHW070606160726

48003CB00005B/2131